**DATE DUE**

| | | | |
|---|---|---|---|
| | | | |
| | | | |
| | | | |
| | | | |
| | | | |
| | | | |
| | | | |
| | | | |
| | | | |
| | | | |

# HOT AS AN ICE CUBE

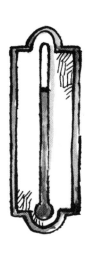

# HOT AS AN ICE CUBE

BY PHILIP BALESTRINO

Illustrated by Tomie de Paola

THOMAS Y. CROWELL COMPANY    NEW YORK

# LET'S-READ-AND-FIND-OUT SCIENCE BOOKS

Editors: *DR. ROMA GANS*, Professor Emeritus of Childhood Education, Teachers College, Columbia University

*DR. FRANKLYN M. BRANLEY*, Chairman and Astronomer of The American Museum–Hayden Planetarium

*Air Is All Around You*

*Animals in Winter*

*A Baby Starts to Grow*

*Bats in the Dark*

*Bees and Beelines*

*Before You Were a Baby*

*The Big Dipper*

*Big Tracks, Little Tracks*

*Birds at Night*

*Birds Eat and Eat and Eat*

*Bird Talk*

*The Blue Whale*

*The Bottom of the Sea*

*The Clean Brook*

*Cockroaches: Here, There, and Everywhere*

*Down Come the Leaves*

*A Drop of Blood*

*Ducks Don't Get Wet*

*The Emperor Penguins*

*Find Out by Touching*

*Fireflies in the Night*

*Flash, Crash, Rumble, and Roll*

*Floating and Sinking*

*Follow Your Nose*

*Giraffes at Home*

*Glaciers*

*Gravity Is a Mystery*

*Green Turtle Mysteries*

*Hear Your Heart*

*High Sounds, Low Sounds*

*Hot as an Ice Cube*

*How a Seed Grows*

*How Many Teeth?*

*How You Talk*

*Hummingbirds in the Garden*

*Icebergs*

*In the Night*

*It's Nesting Time*

*Ladybug, Ladybug, Fly Away Home*

*The Listening Walk*

*Look at Your Eyes\**

*A Map Is a Picture*

*The Moon Seems to Change*

*My Five Senses*

*My Hands*

*My Visit to the Dinosaurs*

*North, South, East, and West*

*Oxygen Keeps You Alive*

*Rain and Hail*

*Rockets and Satellites*

*Salt*

*Sandpipers*

*Seeds by Wind and Water*

*Shrimps*

*The Skeleton Inside You*

*Snow Is Falling*

*Spider Silk*

*Starfish*

*Straight Hair, Curly Hair\**

*The Sun: Our Nearest Star*

*The Sunlit Sea*

*A Tree Is a Plant*

*Upstairs and Downstairs*

*Use Your Brain*

*Watch Honeybees with Me*

*Weight and Weightlessness*

*What Happens to a Hamburger*

*What I Like About Toads*

*What Makes a Shadow?*

*What Makes Day and Night*

*What the Moon Is Like\**

*Where Does Your Garden Grow?*

*Where the Brook Begins*

*Why Frogs Are Wet*

*The Wonder of Stones*

*Your Skin and Mine\**

*AVAILABLE IN SPANISH

L.C. Card 70-139092

ISBN 0-690-40414-X
0-690-40415-8 (Lib. Ed.)

2    3    4    5    6    7    8    9    10

# HOT AS AN ICE CUBE

Everything in the world has heat in it.

The coffee my brother drinks for breakfast has a lot of heat in it. Sometimes it is hot enough to burn you. My sister's bottle of milk has heat in it too. It is warm, but not as hot as my big brother's coffee. There is the same amount of milk in my glass and in the baby's bottle, but her milk has more heat in it.

But my glass of cold milk has heat in it too. So does ice cream. "Cold" does not mean there is no heat.

Even an iceberg at the North Pole has heat in it.

Hot chocolate has a lot of heat. When it cools, there is less heat. It becomes chocolate milk. If the chocolate milk is put in a freezer it becomes frozen chocolate ice. The chocolate milk changed from very hot to freezing cold. This is called a change in temperature. When the temperature of something changes, the amount of heat in it changes too.

Temperature tells you how hot or cold a thing is. An iceberg is cold. It has a low temperature. A fire is hot. It has a high temperature. Hot and cold are words that describe the temperature of something. So are words like warm, lukewarm, chilly, and freezing.

When you heat something its **temperature** rises. What makes this happen?

Everything in the world is made of tiny particles called molecules. Rocks, boats, and ice cream are made of molecules. So are water and milk. You and I are made of molecules too. Things are made of molecules just the way a sand castle is made of grains of sand, except molecules are much smaller. They are really too tiny to see or count.

There are more molecules in one grain of sand than there are grains of sand on the whole beach. There are billions of molecules in **a** single grain of sand.

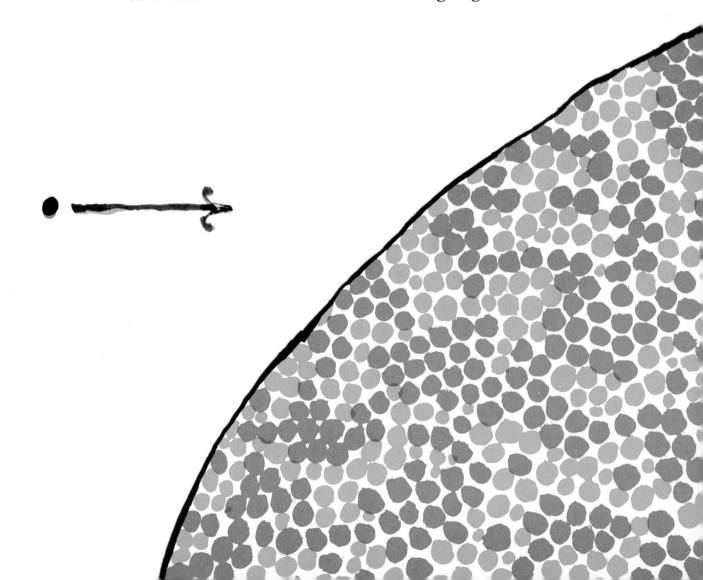

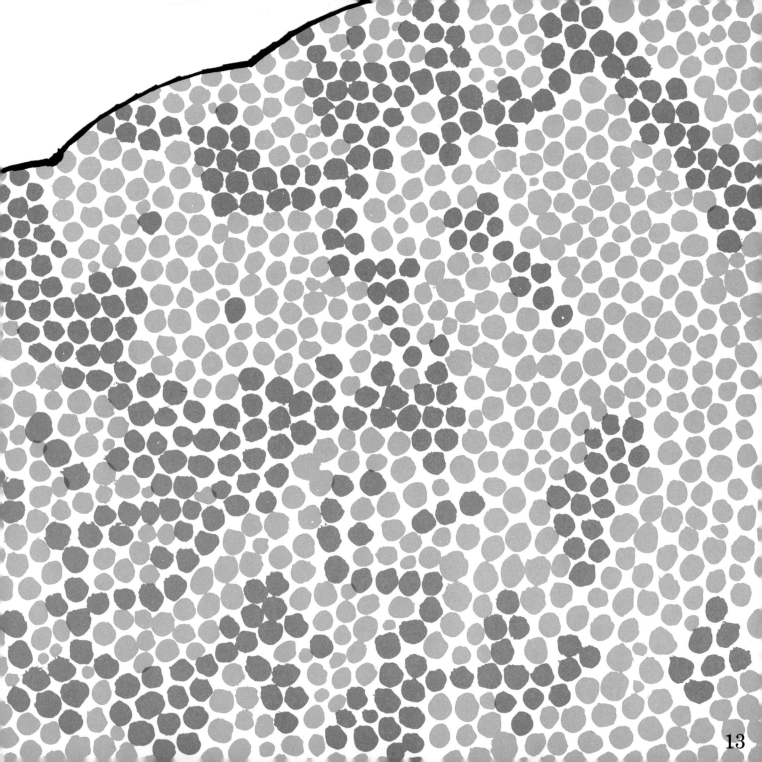

13

Molecules are always moving. They move like pop-corn jumping in a popcorn machine. The faster the molecules in something move, the hotter it is. The molecules of a sizzling hot dog move faster than they do when the hot dog has just come from the freezer.

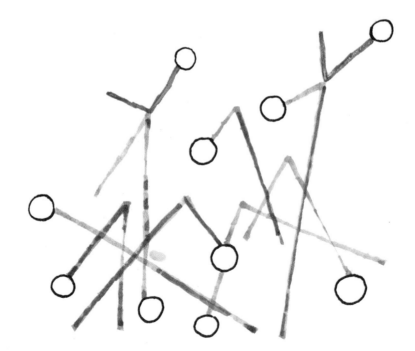

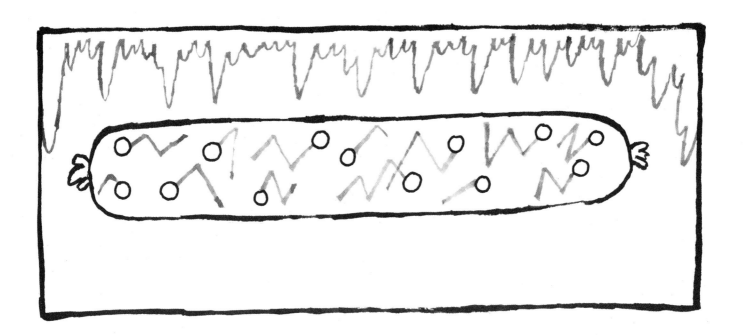

15

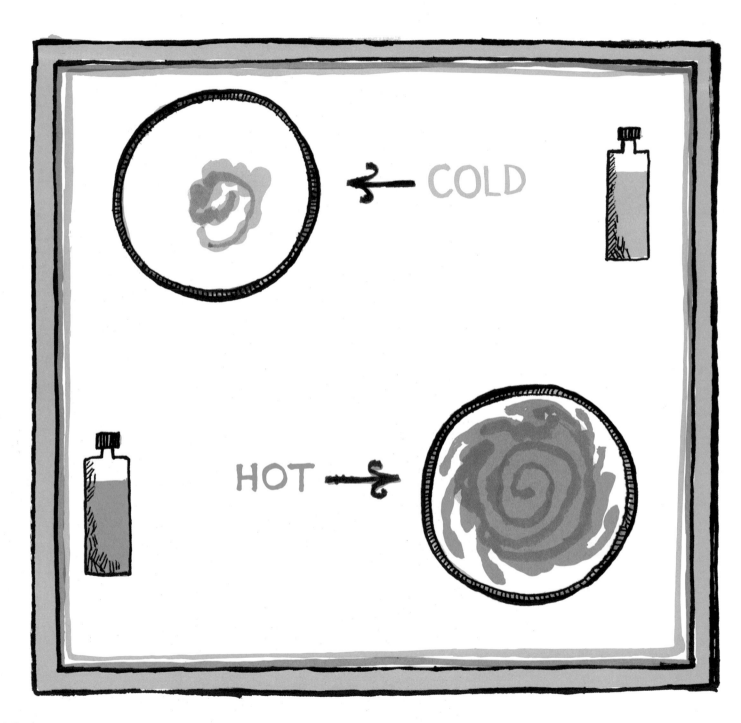

COLD

HOT →

You can see that molecules of water move faster when the water is hotter by doing this experiment. Put water in two bowls: cold water in one bowl, hot water in the other. Let the water sit for a minute so that it is very still. Then carefully put a drop of food coloring into the middle of each bowl. In the cold water, the molecules move the food coloring around only a little bit. In the hot water, they make the food coloring move around a lot faster.

When something hot and something cold are brought together, heat will always move from the hotter thing to the cooler one. Drop some ice cubes in a glass of warm lemonade. The heat from the warm lemonade will go into the ice cubes. The lemonade will be cooler because some of the heat has gone out of it. The ice will melt because heat has gone into it.

Here is another experiment you can do with bowls of water. Fill a bowl half full of ice-cold water. Fill another bowl half full of hot water. Place one hand in the hot water and one hand in the cold water. Leave them there and count to ten.

Before

After

Before

After

One hand will get cold because heat goes from it to the water. The other hand will get hot because heat goes from the water to it. The hot water will now be a little cooler too, and the cold water will be warmer. Can you see why?

The hotter some things get, the larger they become. They expand. At the beach one day my big brother blew up my beach ball, but not all the way up. He left it just a little bit squishy. He said the sun would make the ball expand to its full size.

And it did.

The sun heated the air inside my beach ball. The molecules moved faster. They bounced against the inside of the ball more often and harder. The molecules pushed the ball out to its full size.

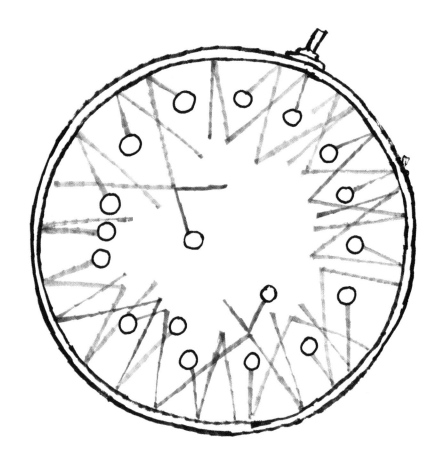

27

In summer, sidewalks expand. The spaces between the squares in sidewalks are put there to let the sidewalks get bigger without cracking. Bridges are longer in summer because heat makes the metal in them expand. Metal in buildings expands too.

The buildings get taller.

As something gets cooler it gets smaller. It contracts because the molecules slow down. When we got home from the beach it was a lot cooler outside. My beach ball was squishy again. And I knew why.

## ABOUT THE AUTHOR

Philip Balestrino is a free-lance writer who lives in Manhattan with an English setter named Derf. Born in Brooklyn, Mr. Balestrino grew up on Long Island and went to college at Bucknell University in Pennsylvania, where he began writing plays for children and for adults. While working toward his master's degree in drama at The Catholic University of America in Washington, D.C., he helped establish a children's theater company for the city's poverty program.

In his leisure time, Mr. Balestrino enjoys exploring New York, collecting antique children's books, and playing long games of Monopoly.

## ABOUT THE ILLUSTRATOR

Tomie de Paola received his Bachelor of Fine Arts degree from Pratt Institute and also studied at the Skowhegan School of Painting and Sculpture, Skowhegan, Maine, under the noted painter Ben Shahn. He holds advanced degrees from the California College of Arts and Crafts and Lone Mountain College in San Francisco.

In addition to illustrating children's books, Mr. de Paola's interests include the theater, cooking, teaching, and traveling. He has had many one-man shows of his prize-winning paintings and drawings, and has also designed Christmas cards, notepaper, and stage sets.

Tomie de Paola now lives in Vermont, where he devotes all his time to writing and illustrating.